THE BATTLE
ANTONY OWEN

KFS
PAMPHLETS

Newton-le-Willows

Published in the United Kingdom in 2022
by The Knives Forks And Spoons Press,
51 Pipit Avenue,
Newton-le-Willows,
Merseyside,
WA12 9RG.

ISBN 978-1-912211-91-3

Acknowledgements:

The author gratefully acknowledges the following literary magazines who published some of the poems in this collection or versions of them: *Surging Tide Magazine, The Journal, Burrow, The Disappointed Housewife, Nightingale, Ink Sweat & Tears, Coven, Fire & Dust, Militant Thistles, Little fires everywhere, Belleville Park Pages.*

As this book goes to print the author gratefully acknowledges plans and support from the following organisations who have pledged to support work from this book and/or awareness of the battles many are facing with mental health: Coventry City FC in the Community, Coventry & Warwickshire MIND, Hillz FM Radio, Positive Images, Lord Mayor of Coventry and many more.

LOTTERY FUNDED

Supported using public funding by
**ARTS COUNCIL
ENGLAND**

For Emily Alice Martha and Joanne

Contents

The Battle   7

Wormholes   8

Winter of 1987   9

Monster   10

Autism Hiding   11

A Sales Manager's Response to Autism   12

My Dad Wants to Meet me for Coffee   13

Adult Autism   14

The Hotel I Planned to Kill Myself In   15

Poem for the Damned   16

John the Alpha   17

Man Up   18

Emergency Sales Meeting   19

When Men Mansplain to Men   20

Phallus   21

Sexual Feelings   22

My Dad Wants to Meet for Coffee Again   23

Why Some People Cannot Forgive Suicide   24

I Put a Sparrow Out of Her Misery   26

What the Woods Taught Me   27

The Great Depression   28

Flat Earth   29

Voles   30

Advice for the Mentally Affected (aka everyone)   31

Little Things to Be Thankful Of   32

Men Speaking Up about Depression and the Alpha Issue ... 33

The Battle

Sorry you have had to wait three years for an assessment.
Perhaps you can take refuge in the colours you emit?
Remember the first time the lads called you a 'spastic',
and take comfort you are special in twenty twenty-one.

Sorry we can only ask how long a piece of string is without metric.
It could be decades, years, months, days for an assessment.
In the meantime, here is a leaflet for a help group in four weeks.
Here is a collective of people just like you, *yet unique.*

Antony Owen

Wormholes

My first wormhole was my 7th Christmas.
I revved my Scalextric car just to smell smoke and despair.
The 911 Porsche smashed into a porcelain ballerina, decapitating her.
I blew into the void of the ballerina's body to create my own noise,
fixed it back on with Airfix glue and studied the cracks I made.
Years later my Mum noticed it was broken and lobbed it out.

I used to have a gaming friend who pushed me too far.
He messed up my tower system of cartridges,
suggesting we sled in the snow outside.
I told him it was the wrong type of snow
and that he was just my Atari friend.
I told him to leave: and that was that.

Someone recently asked me why I never make eye contact.
I told they / them / their that I didn't know how to explain it.
Then compared my eyes to a portal to them rejecting me.
If I were to make a mask out of letters I could explain it in a poem.
If pronouns existed for Asperger's they would be sensory.
The tracers of Scalextric cars coarse as a thistle.

Winter of 1987

Snowfall at fourteen is like a first kiss.
I remember watching the factory turn to Cair Paravel.
The halogen lights of Scandinavian cars aglow like Turkish delight.

For me, the winter of 1987 was like God took a shotgun to the angels.
Their dirty feathers be-felling the pure adolescents
trying their best to avoid the lie and cage.

I thought of digging myself an igloo and drifting away from nurofen.
Three months later I would swallow them like snowflakes –
feeling my down like tawny icicles my unmaker made.

Snow makes everything new for a while. Like a liars promise,
you melt away into those you place your dream.
I was a boy inside a wolf that lost its song.

When my daughter comes of age we shall dissect the snowman
and I shall show her its DNA is made of hands that formed it.
We shall toss the carrot and the hat into the brook and hug.

Antony Owen

Monster

My doctor is wearing a mask.
I am removing all of mine
to reveal who I am:
the muted worker,
the vocal rebel,
a fading boy.

I just called my lockdown Doctor.
She prescribes me potions.
I swallow pills of rain,
gulp government air
and citalopram.
I'm a chemical
Frankenstein.

Autism Hiding

The first book that read me was Robinson Crusoe.
It was the island I connected with, the sea, the wreckage.
When you are a child and called odd you inhabit the sky.
You free sticklebacks in jam-jars because you see factory-men.
This is the sum of their parts – a dead-end river filled with lager cans.

The first girl that kissed me chased me across nettles for my lips.
She asked if she could do so and I asked her why she wanted to.
I remember her Pepto-pink lipstick stained on my cuffs.
Wiping a kiss off your mouth was like pulling wings off an Admiral –
you can almost feel the pop and the beauty leaves scales of a sky-mermaid.

I was never the same as my friends. They were able to leave each day.
Some of us take that line of horizon for its margin of our lost time.
People like me, *but not like me,* in the family of Admirals and Sticklebacks.
We are not to be trapped or pulled apart, *and yet it is our fate.*
If you see such a thing you will want to capture it at least once or kill it over.

In me is such a thing,
autism hiding as some strand of algae –
taking the light, becoming dark for it.
Leave your jam-jars and nets and I may let you see me.

Antony Owen

A Sales Manager's Response to Autism

After exorcising the demon of autism to my boss
she tutted her disappointment at the setback,
reminding me we have targets to meet.
'Do you need special treatment'?
'I could do without this today'!

I could do without my autism every day at work.
People like me project secondary colours.
You cannot mix them into objectives.
Human resources have no resource.
The informal chat is very formal.

This former manager looked like a kind Nan.
She probably was a kind Nan after hours.
She probably adored her grandchildren.
She probably watched *Rain Man* once
and considered herself informed.

My Dad Wants to Meet me for Coffee

My Dad touched me on the knee and spoke:
'we'll have to meet for a coffee sometime'.
I did not have the heart to tell him,
because I did not feel my heart to tell him
that my heart is in my stomach these days,
and he is the cocoon where my butterflies breed.

Antony Owen

Adult Autism

Before I was special
I was an angel in formaldehyde.
I was a minotaur with bulging bollocks.
I was Perseus versus Medusa trapping her in my shield.

Now I am special
I am a jar of pickles prickling the palate.
I am a Roman statue the Visigoths defaced –
its penis severed, dusting the pink roses vulva.

The Hotel I Planned to Kill Myself In

My suicide note was going to be a timed email
scheduled to send the moment I became born.
I had hoped to trick God this way,
to swallow spring water with pills,
leave a part of me pure for hell.

My suicide was going to be in a rundown hotel,
yet the sun would have risen on my cold body
and moon would have kissed me goodnight.
I had planned a Spotify list to listen to –
to drift off into the woodwind place
thinking of faces I loved.

My second suicide note was to the chambermaid.
They would have found me all twisted up
like a lightning tree disgracing wind.
They would have needed therapy,
five minutes to turn the room:
we all have targets to meet.

My wife saved me with her ears taking this all in.
The colour from her face slid into the nothing.
The tears from her eyes fell into full stops,
the beat from her heart sprinting
to save me from the other me.

Antony Owen

Poem for the Damned

In the empty ward I lay there full of paracetamol.
A nurse stroked my hair like a bow on a broken cello.
The music of my mother's yowl destroyed my father.

I searched inside myself and found a great hallway of a viola.
Above were wild horses tied to a bow of bone.
I can turn words into octaves here and rest.

Outside, the stars burnt like Ortolan's in black brandy.
Should I cover my head in shame with a towel,
not to offend God at innocence so morbidly devoured?

I have this dream where my inner child buffers into a person.
He is trying to tune into me smacking the screen for a picture.
I can see him through the glass but I am invisible to him.

I had this recurring fantasy of a grandfather clock my dad liked.
I'd rip out its throat and set about smashing its face in.
The clocks hands are no more capable of chimes.

Oh, Holy Father and earthly Father, I have offended you.
My untimely Amen was not a psalm or prayer.
It was all for me and the black Doberman.

John the Alpha

At the teams meeting in the pub
John singled me out for drinking a Macchiato.
I said I liked coffee and he whispered: *'yeah and cock too'*.

Daz got promoted outside. Emerging from Marlboro mist
he said: *'it was high time Karen got a kick in the cunt
for taking his accounts, she would pay big time'*.

John arranged a motivation session paint-balling.
He arrived with camouflage under his eyes.
Told me he was going to shoot Karen.

Someone spread a rumour that Karen shagged John.
She went to human resources to feel human.
John rang his wife begging her to stay.

Antony Owen

Man Up

In the guillotine of stratus
nights head dropped bloody
and I thought of my friend hanging.

My boss said he's worried about me.
How everyone else has seen it too.
He sent me a gif to remind me I'm only human.

My friend died in a ropes eye.
She loved horses, so an apt departure:
her neck galloping in horsehair.

My boss told me it's been three weeks,
that it's time to man up and hit target.
I told him *'I'm only human'* to his face.

Emergency Sales Meeting

In the sired group
a silverback strutted, punching a number from thin air.
Singling out Adam, he analogised his failure to Cov being relegated.
A woman started to cry and he offered her a custard cream and a cliché.

Past the marble reception the silverback stuck a number on the toilet wall.
He made a joke that when people shit themselves they can see why.
He said that Adam is on the last rung to the hangman's noose.
He asked me how my poetry is going, and sniggered.

Adam went on the sick.
His partner, Darren, met the silverback.
I heard his stare so loud into the silverback's eyes,
followed by a warning as the ape retreated hastily to HR.

Antony Owen

When Men Mansplain to Men

A man once told me I would never make it as a serious poet .
He said, *'beware Kerouac was a drunk and dreamer'*.
I immediately read Kerouac and the beats.

A poet once told me that I should go to an Arvon class to learn poetry.
The following year I went to Hiroshima instead.
I saw Kerouac on sale translated into Kanji.

Phallus

It is not alpha or advisable
for a man to admit erectile problems,
but here I am anyway: the shame of Priapus and real men.

I was once told to Man-up on a jolly by a millennial go-getter.
He gave me advice on how to close a deal,
his bumfluff beard dancing in the wind.

I am having problems getting hard.
I am having problems feeling any sense of love.
You cannot make love if you're depressed or half a man.

My friend warned me against going public with this,
he said once it's printed I can't go back. But then,
he also once said that only weirdoes write poems.

Antony Owen

Sexual Feelings

I touch-screened endless categories to feel something –
couldn't find lovers, just Milf and Anal.
I have no sexual feelings.

I have no feelings.
The dark sides of daily moons I swallow
are anti-depressant, anti-human.

This level of honesty is not to be encouraged, is it?
Someone will say I am oversharing.
Jill from HR will be in touch.

What is touch anyway?

My Dad Wants to Meet for Coffee Again

Perhaps I should soften like April light on the hardy plants.
That is my attempt at creating a metaphor out of my dad,
and I can do better than that, but poets are sometimes arseholes.

Perhaps I should learn from the condensation in a bouquet
and understand that cut down carnations in their prime have a beauty
that is a metaphor for me – and I am trying so hard not to be an arsehole.

My Dad wants to meet for coffee again and has thrown in he will pay.
It is tempting to take him up on the offer and meet him in Costa.
It is tempting like Amsterdam windows, but I'll probably regret it.

My Dad is getting older. The light never returns from his wrinkles.
He glows from the inside, making his liver spots resemble paper burning.
Perhaps I'll meet my dad for coffee and I'll sit by the papers just in case.

My Father lathed moving parts for cars and a stillness of childhood.
He was the man who plucked blackthorns from my hands.
One of them nicked my lifeline and I loved him like soft April rain for it.

Antony Owen

Why Some People Cannot Forgive Suicide

'I've no sympathy for your friend who killed herself, she had a kid for fucks sake'

— **Ex work colleague**

I remember as a teenager the yelping of my mother in shock
as if her kit had started suckling milk then ripped her apart.
I learnt that night how certain tears sting like pretty hemlock.

That night, retching up codeine, I felt the embers of my Mum's lifeline
standing over me wiping casseroled chicken from my chin.
Later, I saw her feet kissing the lip of my door, her cracked breath.

I remember my little brother's child eyes rash-red from weeping.
His slow-mo words, I tried to block out, that ricocheted.
He grew up that day – and that was my murder.

Looking back, I remember my father in the mist of his moped.
Dragging the laments of factory life with him to my bones.
We camped there for a while in the wigwam of our skin.

I remember first day back at school to news of my failure.
My best friend's throat swallowing the weight of unmanly grief.
We never spoke a word about it until we thought we were men.

I loved them more than ever, yet after I was lost even more.
Not going through with suicide provokes the inner ghost;
it is just a pause and one day the Ouija of touch may summon it.

I get why people cannot forgive suicide: there is no answer;
there is no answer to being incapable of joy and pain;
there is no answer to a normal day *then the act.*

I read of a wife who found her husband hung in the garage.
She described him as a pendulum stopping time itself.
Ten years on she wants to forgive, but cannot.

I get why some people ghost the demons that haunt them.
As a son I was the elephant in the room and circus.
And now, as a father, I know how it is to be child and ghost.

And now, in the perfect circle of my unlit séance,
I walk out the circle and into the world.
I forgive no one or ask for it.

Antony Owen

I Put a Sparrow Out of Her Misery

My cat broke the wing of a sparrow.
It flew into boomerang curves,
arriving back to its talon.

I put a sparrow out of her misery,
it flew kited with its intestines –
bunting for a cold creator.

What the Woods Taught Me

I was born in the clouds. My mother
left dew all over her quaking landscape.
She held me up in our atmospheres and claimed me.

We lived in the otherworld of steel and sweat.
My Dad trying to decode the alpha workplace –
awkward as a runt nudged from the numbered tits.

Everything was made for us and given names –
the house, the car, my Nan sent home to perish,
her last words spoken in morphine nonsense.

I used to go to the woods to be repaired by birds.
The robin never wanted me. I liked her honesty.
A horse sidled my lifelines and held me in its eyes.

The woods taught me how the earth is like skin.
What matters is all that lies beneath you and I.
That skin is just the hemisphere of something near to a soul.

I remember my old roommate wrote *'this cannot be my clams'*.
He swam in bottles of Glenfiddich and died in the peat.
They called him an addict, but they didn't understand our street.

I remember my Nan with fags stuffed down her tights,
fresh from being let out by hospital without pants on,
she took that bent Rothmans out with such grace and lit it.

I want to take a hammer to the plug sockets on my wall.
Rip out the tendons and switch off the telly.
Switch off the world that left moths in my belly.

I want to dig up my Nans bones and hold them in swaddling,
take them to the woods and throw them in the stream,
and watch clouds lift where the waterfall sighs at peace.

Antony Owen

The Great Depression

After 'The Hare Refuses to Speak' by Wendy Pratt

A hearse of rooks pauses sky
and I picture Holden folding the rye
searching for children ill-fated to die.

I will Karcher the lichen from tombs
to record the forgotten in cold stone wombs
that break through earth in vivid blooms.

I once grieved an embryo that never formed.
The lamplit walls of my wife never warmed
a dead nest still from nothing that swarmed.

I think of my body as Alaska in spring.
The soft mouth of a fox with a guillemot's wing.
Its zoomed out pupils as its bell-heart rings.

Flat Earth

I laid on the world,
Kissed the back of her neck.
That yellow thicket no longer rises.
I am less sexual a being after black dogs.
Growing older you stop shedding skins and consume yourself.

I watched the world explode.
I must be so exhausting at times.
My mind sashays from all compass points.
I start things and ~~do not~~ cannot finish them.
My heart is a goblet of guilt for this metamorphosis I never chose.

Antony Owen

Voles

Blackbird composes my sliver of sky.
These disputes calm my prison of three:
I see branches in my skin, a tree, am I?

At dark-fall I watched a slipknot of starlings
threading through the pinprick sun like a wound.
My world is folding inward with every wing.

Tonight I drink whiskey until I float above us.
Still as a kestrel I accept the winds of change.
I am so high we are all so small, like petrified voles.

Advice for the Mentally Affected (aka everyone)

In Las Vegas they give you a suite if you gamble.
You can watch ninety-six channels of America dying.
You can watch desert sunsets struggle through logos,
and in the morning you play golf on mafia graves.

In England they gamble your mental health at number ten.
You can watch the little people morph into Lowry sticks,
walking without faces chained to shadows coming loose.
Everyone is being buried in clear view by elected gangsters.

I have some advice for the mentally affected –
look up over the rooftops until you only see clouds.
Elect the utopia of sky and avalanche of cumulus.
Take a deep breath and walk until only your calves are heavy.

Antony Owen

Little Things to Be Thankful Of

Above the crimes
a pylon can redeem us
through birdsong necklaces
tied around the slit throat dusk.

Above the white world
night can wind a tannoy of wolves.
Even in the city their lights can be seen.
One wove between cars in Toronto like a silver ribbon.

Above the new man born a girl
everything is changing in the sky.
Covid has cleaned the Boeing traces of man.
A flock of geese breaks formation for a Walmart drone.

Below all this is me and you.
At night I hang my skins over the ottoman,
turn into a blur when I am creature like and loving.
Sometimes, but less so now, our shapes converge into one.

Men Speaking Up about Depression and the Alpha Issue …

Around 2017/18 there was a spate of incidents on the track as I was catching the train home that would hold me up before or after an event, sometime you found out later someone had committed suicide. After a failed marriage in the mid noughties, further indiscretions with the lover I was with by the late noughties and leading up to my role as Birmingham Poet Laureate I went through bouts of depression, guilt and not feeling worthy of living, I often walked close to railway tracks, felt the torrent wind of a passing train, serenading me to jump.

Birmingham Snow Hill train station was my favourite haunt, it has a multi-storey car park above it, where back then you could walk to the edge and jump off on the North side on to the tracks, (you'd have to negotiate a fence but it's doable). On the west side there's equally an easy jump on to the streets. I can't tell you how many times with Miles Davis Sketches of Spain, especially the second track El amor brujo (Love, the Magician or The Bewitched Love) I walked close to the edge; sometimes we can be bewitched and in love with depression or the desire to commit suicide.

– Roy McFarlane

After I read a post by Antony on Facebook in November 2021, I got in touch. In the U.K., the group most likely to commit suicide are young men aged between 20 and 49. In 2016, in the midst of a mid-life crisis and the breakdown of my marriage, I was nearly one of those statistics. I had bought a pipe to put over my car exhaust and was saving up anti-depressants that would have put me to sleep. Had I followed through, my two children would have been left without a father. Fortunately, I came through those dark months, but it was very difficult. I spent time in a refuge for people who were suicidal. I was very depressed. I had no motivation. I thought my life was over. With the help of friends and a terrific therapist I came through it, and my life is much better. We need more men to talk about their experiences. We also need to challenge the current climate that demonises male behaviour, imperfect as it is. Shaming men is unhelpful. Most of all, men need to talk more about what matter to them – their hopes, fears and concerns. The culture of men not talking about emotion is doing us no favours. I salute Antony for his work in this area.

– Miles Salter (Writer and Musician)

It is hard to know how to steer a course between the various forms of guilt men have been presented with in the last fifty years, from *All men are bastards*, and *All men are rapists*, through the entire act of sex being regarded as rape (by Andrea Dworkin among others) as well as the countless ills of the world for which men as a gender are held to blame (I have a very long list of links to press articles of that sort that I collected before I got bored of it).

Guilt, shame, and humiliation are weapons against which men have minimal defence. And of course there are always things to be guilty of and shamed for, and a small pile of these can easily be inflated to something oppressively mountain-size. The great increase in male suicide and the expansion of men's groups including MGTOW and Incels are some of the by-products.

The American Psychological Association regards stoicism as a toxic element in males, but I can't see many alternatives to stoicism. *Grin and bear it*, is OK if you bear it with wit. And remember the wonderfully ironic advice and unconscious compliment conferred by: *Man up!*

Poets are not special kinds of men or women: they are people (both men and women) with a gift for language, a feeling for shape, and a spirit of enquiry into the quality of moments, sometimes of the apparently most unpromising sort. As an outstanding female poet, Deryn Rees-Jones titled her selected poems: *What It's Like To Be Alive*.

Manning up for a poet involves facing life not only in terms of our own lives but in terms of the life around us. It is not a matter of gestures and declarations and certainly not self-pity but of an exactitude of terms arising out of a sharp ear for the currents of language. Hold your ear to the membrane of language. Feel its pulse. Feel its wit. Feel its dignity. Sense its shape.

Forget about winning. Forget about glamorising yourself into soaring birds or anything else. Work harder. Fail better. That is where you are. Now work on with who you are.

– George Szirtes

I worked in an office 10 years ago processing sales orders. I felt very anxious calculating quotes from the day that I started but struggled on for a few months thinking I must not quit or I will be considered as weak. One Monday morning I finally snapped. I walked out that day without working my notice. I was accused of 'lacking character and letting my colleagues down' by my boss. I was diagnosed with bipolar disorder shortly afterwards and to this day I struggle with low self-esteem and trust issues. Walking away from the toxic culture of that company was one of the bravest decisions I have made.

– Craig, Stoke, Coventry, 48 years old.

'Being neurodivergent while Black, my being 'man enough' has often been questioned, pertinently someone who writes poetry and does not like cars or sports.

When those who look like you have often rejected you based on disability, it reminds me that masculinity in Black communities has qualifiers attached, where my Blackness is subject to being in closer proximity to white heteropatriarchal imaginings of men (even from other Black men).

In my quest for belonging, this marginalisation from (mainly cishet) Black men has caused bouts of depression, but now in my mid-twenties, I am grateful to have started to find those that look like me who accept me for who I am in all parts of my humanness (it's just taken over twenty years).'

– Tré Ventour, Academic-Poet and Race/Black History Educator

Some remain silent and ride out the black wave until it passes, others are not so lucky, you can never reason with a black dog no matter how many times he takes a bite, in society we are supposed to be stoic, invincible men, we should be statues of strength, and show no weakness, that's how society has built the perception that only the strong survive, it's a type of societal Darwinism, though behind the strong mask the clay is slowly cracking into a silent scream that only one person can hear

– Matt Duggan

As a man it disheartens me that a woman crosses a street at night to avoid passing me, when I knew I meant no harm – thought 'not all men'. Before #MeToo spun out, I thought a woman would have to be very unlucky to have experienced something that gives them every reason to be fearful of any man. It became apparent that terrifying and often prolonged experiences are only too common for most women and as a man the best thing I can do is cross the street and remove any fear as soon as possible. Being disheartened doesn't really compare to being fearful of even going out.

– Martin Figura

For many years, I had depression and anxiety, and as a result, struggled with what my sense of self was. But it was men, through bonding, by helping to strengthen my mental resolve, who guided me out of my morass of despair and worthlessness, as well as help that renewed my sense of purpose

– Chris, 40

Madness is not a curse and the real curse is failing to reach out to those battling with mental illness.

– Rangzeb Hussain

When I was 16, I was bullied at school to the extent I had to leave. I wouldn't fight; partly because I knew I would be rubbish at it but also because I did not want to be like that. Fortunately, I found other people for whom fighting wasn't their identity.

– Mark